OF CERTAIN ANGELS

OF CERTAIN ANGELS

David Harsent

DARE-GALE PRESS

First published in Great Britain by Dare-Gale Press, 2022

Dare-Gale Press, 15-17 Middle Street, Brighton BN1 1AL

www.daregale.com

Distributed by Central Books.

ISBN 9780993331176

Poems © David Harsent, 2022

Thanks are due to *One Hand Clapping* in which 'The Angel of Transformative Light' first appeared.

All rights reserved. No part of this publication may be reproduced, stored in a retrieval system or transmitted, in any form or by any means, electronic, mechanical, photocopying, recording or otherwise without the prior permission of the copyright holder and the publisher.

Cover photograph by Daniel M Nagy.

Font: Typeset in 10/11pt Delicato, designed by Stefan Hattenbach.

Printed in England by TJ Books on munken paper certified by the Forest Stewardship Council.

Dare-Gale Press is committed to carbon neutral and environmentally conscious publishing. For our environmental policy please visit www.daregale.com.

To Julia Rose Gale

Jeder Engel ist schrecklich. Und dennoch, weh mir,
ansing ich euch, fast tödliche
                    Rilke: *Second Duino Elegy*

The Angel of Transformative Light

On her back, on the bed, arms raised, legs spread,
who did this, who dashed on a smudge
of lipstick, fanned her hair across the pillow, guessed

her wingspan, found a way to make a shadow's shadow
from the hard stark white of pinion feathers
against Egyptian cotton, who thought to allow that fusion

of lust and prayer, that fission, eyebright, fever-race,
then bring you in, a ponderous silhouette... *O!*
who gifted her the seven words now cut into your arm

ragged like a prison-house tattoo, who picked the lock
on this door of all doors, who set the cheval glass just so
to give her back to herself, up on all fours, that wide wingspread

mantling her smile and hiding her greed from God? Slow light
when she moves on you like that, smoke-light, water-light.
Leaving, she turns to share a soundless whisper,

a secret lost, white breath on empty air... *O!* in the full flush
of her nakedness, faint scent of fallen ash, walls scuffed
with light, her handprint at the cave-mouth.

The Angel of Lost Things

A Skara Brae of the mind, where she walks
from sun to shade... on either side, stone shelves
where what you thought lost is kept, each *item* bearing

the ache of estrangement, a ghost-limb, each
having forgotten the name it's known by and what it's for:
bric-a-brac set away from the island light

to keep it from spoil. This thumbstone will never
come back to you, but will be as it was in the moment
it fell from sight. If you sometimes reach for it

in memory, you'll bring a fingertip to her backbone.
All given over to chance: that loss-on-loss
is breakage in the pattern of your life: she keeps

a record, something much like a star-chart,
tide-table, notation of birdsong. If only you knew
what prayers and hallelujahs light the commonplace

and why she conjured up these low rooms, lintel and latch
under a scrim of turf and sand, to put the lost things in place
as if she had scavenged them from the tideline

and brought them safe home. There they wait,
suddenly mysterious, palm-prints of claim and protection
pressed to the ceiling-space. Goodwife-angel, she has them set by.

The Angel of the Surrogate Quotidian

As your lover throws back the sheet, unhurried
nakedness, walks to the window soft-footed, sees
a jay gather light to its wingspread, wingspread

of the angel (remember) who brought tokens, a sea-
washed pebble, holly, a handspan of driftwood, and sang
something known only to her that carried a depth

of mourning: grace to the new day's dead. In her satchel
bread, olives, wine. When she sets out that offering
her hands shape the air: a blessing; her wings

mantle the food as a hawk mantles its prey, opening
songbird or shrew, protocols of bloodspill, flesh
as sacrament (remember) bare bones to the wind.

As a man starts a fire in his garden. As rain shapes itself
to urban yards. As a cat goes between glance and glance
to arrive in the moment it leaves, beauty-in-stealth of Noh:

she offers herself to this, to the faint, half-expected
pain behind your eyes, to the ectopic beat, to the way
a stalled breath leaves you trapped in faultless silence.

Your lover turns from the window (remember) and lays
a hand to your face. She offers herself. Of course,
there is singing somewhere close. She is matched to the music.

The Angel of Delinquent Poetries

She has you by heart and gives you back to yourself
in those few moments when she comes to lie beside you,
when you touch her, when your touch puckers her skin,

when she half-turns to speak and her wings gather evening light
setting a shadow-clutter on the wall. (The wall is innocent
of all else.) She has found the damaged music in your lines

and sings it without fault: image and abstract
telling the pale processional of your life. Sometimes
she reframes it to sing of herself: womb-envy, night-vigils,

the debt she is owed by God: a better poem than yours;
it questions flesh and what flesh brings to love, then stops
on a broken note, a woman, suppose she were a woman, stifled.

This poetry is ruinous: her face a map of scars, her wings
crow-black, her fearsome waking dreams of Paradise: a legend
among her kind, its windows and mirrors, roads drawn

to a vanishing-point, white skies, a driven silence.
She harvests cancelled lines, abandoned drafts, those words
that carry more weight of pain than the poem could hold:

fragments of a songline that brought you here
unknown, unknowing, abandoned to chance,
the timelock on your life coded to her palm-print.

The Angel of Death Knell Chorales

Bloodless, blue-lipped, head shaved, is how you see her.
She brings with her, from that other place,
the voices of children, harmony-in-heartbreak

bright notes ringing bare bones, in measure of pain
unmistakeable: a boy treble set against
a muffled bell: her sure hand fills and shapes it.

The descant is rainfall. They sing – she sings –
for Shelley drowned and burned at Viareggio,
Lamia in his pocket: Trelawney caught up his heart

from the brands; she sings – they sing – for Paul Celan,
in off the Pont Mirabeau and washed into a weir;
they sing – she sings – for Hart Crane, numb

to poetry (meaning as good as dead) spectacular
in flight among the birds mobbing the boat.
Will someone, you wonder, *ever catch up my heart?*

The Angel of Cureless Anhedonia

A painting in which she gathers a shawl of nettles to her throat;
a poem where she is made barren by longing; this duet
for alto and sax, marked *lachrimoso* – sadness

as rhythm and flow, as slippage of colour, a word
spoken in slow repeat, soon becoming meaningless,
an errant smile developing toneless laughter...

She enters by rain-light and draws you in. She has a black
book on you: notes of how accidental pleasure
left you staring back at yourself from a shopfront window,

of a letter to someone unnamed, asking to be told again
of coming ashore on that island known for its music
and sunsets, of leaf-shadow on clouded glass

that first morning, of flame kindling the tip of your cigarette
as you lift the perfect martini. (In that same book
is a sketch of you on your knees in simple light.) She sleeps

at the foot of your bed and when you wake at the dead
hour, speaks to you as to a man on a ledge stranded,
as she is stranded, between heaven and earth, and set to fly.

The Angel of Risk and Regret

Airborne in a stairwell or taking a blind bend dead
drunk across the cats'-eyes: her wild laughter
as she laid a hand on the wheel and brought you back:

same hand that held you steady as you stepped
out on the parapet, when to walk on air
with river lights cutting the darkness was to set

risk against anger – and the urge to nudge you over
a ghost-gesture in her: to let you hold your line
on a midnight road, or prompt a curse to a homicidal stare:

the impulse to sin of the harlot-saint, some trace of lust
the desert sun could not burn off. That vision corrupts.
It takes her to the edge. She walks on air.

The Angel of Furtive Eschatologies

Hand-in-hand to the boneyard, that half-heard
seamless note – the city's tinnitus – gone
as if she'd flipped a switch, nothing between you

and the image she allows of the bloodless dead
clawing their coffin lids. The thought amuses her,
just as she smiles at headless stone angels

in the rising mist, at 'TIS DEATH IS DEAD NOT SHE,
at the drum-roll of thunder that celebrates your arrival.
She calls on the dead for a dance

which you somehow see, subtle music in bones
as they go between markers that bear their names,
until she sends them back. None of this is cruel:

as you remember the dead so the dead
remember you: things are what they are: she allows
sight of them whole and undisturbed, or their wounds

showing livid and wet, or a bar-code of illness
die-stamped at the quick, or where
they gain themselves, remade, in the sight of God.

Now, in this dry storm, faux-apocalypse, you tremble
to join the dance. She will play for you on a bone aulos.
On the way back she will touch you, softly, to slow your heart.

The Angel of Stopless Sorrow

At this time of night, in this depth of darkness, the house
brings in the sound of someone weeping, weeping
and sometimes speaking, that low music fading

to a single note as you go from room to room
where the voice left traces, so you collect
syllables that rearrange to *end of days* or *flood and fire*.

Here is what would be her footprint, what would be
her image on glass, a shed feather, the shape
she would make in air: unmistakeable for its stoop: the line

from lowered head to breast to hip to knee
sorrow's golden mean. Now take her scent, nightstock,
tart like her yearly bleed; she draws you on

as if gesture could pattern the silence. In one account
she is dark-eyed and reckless, in another a dove tamed to the dovecote.
Her burden is inexpressible love. She has forgotten your name.

The Angel of the Skyborne Mirage

She catches you in the corner of her eye and reinvents you
as a refugee soul in need of some measure of love,
drawing you in and into the scope of her wings,

the close edge of passion, her body dark angles and deep
scents in which you might suffocate:
that feather-cradle, that aphrodisiac musk... The mirage

only sustains by your belief in her and hers in you:
sometimes cloudwrack, unfallen rain, patterns of light
refracting to a hall of mirrors that returns you to yourself

as victim or lover or starveling or vengeful child,
sometimes a web of streets abandoned
to patterns of light that blur to reachless distance,

sometimes a long perspective of rivers and bridges,
skies pearl and featureless, the water showing patterns
of light and the image of a man in torn reflections.

She works these changes, and more, in God's delay.
If you find ash on the heel of your shoe
you have come back (be sure) to where you most belong.

The Angel of Venereal Nocturnes

Stay close: when birdsong dies her song comes in
on a single breath, and you think water-flow, or how
still air is stirred by flight. Her voice is low

and holds a seamless note that trips your heart,
the burden sin-through-pleasure, the line-by-line much like
some black-book version of the marriage vow.

She stoops to bring you on, her gaze held hard
as a lover might set a dare, and the song, as it leaves her,
falls to flesh and the Devil, her secrets and yours caught up

in that slow music, your memory and hers of desire, of risk,
of betrayal both pure and simple. She will sing into remembrance
the girl with the rosary, on her knees by firelight,

or the other, good with knives at the kitchen counter, or
the garden goddess looking up to your sun-glossed window,
blood-beads plucked on her skin by the churn of bramble.

Tokens, touchstones, a sacred heart on the sill, a fish clean-scaled
and slit from nock to gill, blood-beads smudged
onto the palms of your hands. And now she has you on stall:

your suddenly empty eye, your indrawn breath, her song
a pendulum, illusions of aphrodisia, of morning-light
in the room where she first found you alone and terrified.

The Angel of White Silences

In the world's turning there comes a moment of stall,
earth's apnoea, when the unborn and the new-dead
gather a silence: it is all she knows of Heaven.

Silence as the knife is taken up, as water
grows still, as hope turns back, as thought
shuts down, as a door closes never to be opened.

The perfect lie in its cage of silence, the dropped
heartbeat that marks the wedding-vow, the bird
as it catches rising air (*O!* she is at your shoulder:

half turn, her breasts graze your arm, you see how well
she carries her scar), an echo – your name – emptied
into itself, that nerveless silence which is the silence

of the mad, a dream narrative broken, a word
in the mouth of the unearthed skull, a man
in the soundless acres of his leap from the parapet.

'Find me out in that last moment' (your whispered prayer)
'You will never find me penitent, but find me out
in the deep white silence of my death where I come to nothing.'

At the still centre, her vision holds: of fire
on the sea, fire at the core, at the end of the ending day,
silence of a dying star as it folds to whiteness, she waits on this.

The Angel of the Good Death

She brings to a white room a white bed. Full moon
to the bare window. White silence to empty walls.
A white book, your last and best, lies where it fell.

She is wearing one of the lost things: a jet
choker retrieved from the rack of days
when the near-world dimmed and words

shed their meanings and memory turned on itself.
She waits in the room. Hers is the only scent: a thin
reek, which is desire, which is death-sweat,

her gift to you when the time is right.
That white light, a pin-spot, comes from her diadem:
if you were here it would find you centre-stage,

a man self-abandoned, speechless, blind, holding
a vision of fire on the skim of the sea, holding a line
of music, uprooted, that plays back and back again.

She will come with whisky when you call for it.
She will come to you naked in the small hours.
She will come to your funeral, as promised, *en deuil blanc.*